SWIMMING IN WORDS

New and Selected Poems

Luke Icarus Simon

STIRLING
PUBLISHING
AUSTRALIA

First published 2024 by Stirling Publishing Australia

Enquiries should be made to the publisher:
stirlingpublishingaustralia@gmail.com

National Library of Australia cataloguing-in-publication data
Is available at http://catalogue.nla.gov.au

ISBN (pbk) 978 0 99 451 82 62
ISBN (hardcover) 978 0 99 451 82 86
ISBN (ebk) 978 0 99 451 82 79

Cover art design: Hazel Lam
Designed and typeset in (Garamond 11/20pt) by Luke Harris
Headings 11pt Proxima Nova Wide
At Working Type Studio,
PO BOX 72 Eltham, Victoria 3095

Dedicated to my three siblings

Also by Luke Icarus Simon

POETRY

Latin

The Transit of Cancer

The Gospel of the Fallen: Selected Poems 1996-2006

NOVEL

The Art In My Palm

SHORT STORIES

Lost In The Last Divided Capital

PLAYS

Urban Tales of Utter Devotion

Fish Wednesday

Sir

A House On An Island In the Aegean

NON-FICTION

Michael Gow: A Thematic Approach

The Little Book On How To Stop Smoking

SCREENPLAYS

My Stamp Collection (ABC TV)

Schism (AFTRS)

English At Work (SBS TV- 3 episodes)

About the poet

Luke Icarus Simon was born and raised in Cyprus.

Since the early 1980s, his poetry and short stories have been widely published in literary journals, anthologies and magazines in Australia and overseas.

His most recent theatre play was produced at Melbourne's *La Mama* in 2021.

He lives in a small town along the Murray River in NSW, Australia.

Contents

THE CRIMES OF A SIMPLE MAN

Sucking
strawberries in Santiago
mid November
the flavour is all enticing
everyone seems to be
speaking Spanish

Appearances are the go,
the surface   aspirational
classe ejecutiva, plato ejecutivo, piso ejecutivo
four-year-olds hand out written messages of begging
get angry if they do not receive   if you refuse
to contribute to their exploitation   their misery

In the Parisian avenues of Las Condes
an expectation of something wonderful about to happen
but nothing happens
walk a couple of blocks
another country altogether
You can be killed for your shoes

An isolated existence
We don't look beyond that hill
wine to tempt the gods
a place where minor films turn into controversies
a priest has sex too for god's sake
shock horror

All wanting Pinochet back
taxi drivers sing his praises
educated *universitarios* too
He built this country
made us work, bought us cars
We are masochists, a waiter tells me straight

Give me the whip I say
I shall crack it hard
the priest can bend over too
I will get even then
He too is just a man
My mother would say.

LOVE LATINO STYLE

What do you mean, my feelings aren't important?

At private universities they listen to black rap
rock pesado sells bucket-loads, their hair long, unwashed
(they have no idea about the lyrics)
I am told they hate English and loathe *gringos*

He insists
he's extremely discreet, has to be
an only son of ageing parents, his father is ill
a former general living in Parral now

Meanwhile...
the grapevine assures me
he performs publicly and openly in trios
with his new boyfriend at the sauna most weekends

At the five-star hotel where the hot water is tepid
they expect a *propina* just as they breathe
for doing nothing more
than the minimum required by their job

In the efficient Metro they are slow n' sweaty
miserable masochists reading free newspapers
suffocating in the smog, in the hypocrisy
they have created

The women kiss you but
never invite you home for an empanada
in the safe space inside my head
he loves me passionately, intensely

His black eyes encompassing the totality
of my soul
of the entire riches of the world
his Chilean dialect, his voice soothes

In real life
he has abused me
without touching me
like a ten-thousand-*peso* whore

In the hotel room
I watch Hollywood scandals on cable
in the boxy flats of the city
no one ever returns your call

But every man and homeless dog
owns a mobile
(a *cellular,* but they hate Americans, right?)
I keep hearing my dead mother's voice here…

High above on San Cristobal
the Italian marble beams
day and night until four am
the time I am alone   restless

Providing a point of reference
an aspect of love
an immaculate hope
to all who are deprived.

THE MAN WAS SOMETHING LIKE THE TITLE OF AN ABBA SONG

New Year's Day is always difficult
all that kissing of strangers the night before
too much cheap alcohol flowing too much naked
flesh showing   never seeing those bloody fireworks

You feel guilty
for not visiting the grave
her final resting place
the graves of all those pathetic adolescent dreams

I used to give press conferences
on the toilet seat
when I could still imagine
a better welcoming of the year ahead

How many times can you beg?
Dime que me quieres,
*(*how many languages do I have to learn?*)*
his withheld love is all you need on this day

Funny
but on the telephone with fifteen hours' difference
it is easy to simply say
how he makes you feel exquisitely special

"*Me too*" sounds so much more
sincere in Spanish
meanwhile the dog's hungry
the garden's a mess

The barren marital bed
is neatly made
crisp   a show home
untouched.

TASTE IT

First day of autumn   southern hemisphere
messy maple leaves   curled up   dead in the courtyard
the air recalcitrant   the mood reminiscent
of the smell of a nineteen year-old's body
of my mother's potato and leek egg-lemon soup

The pungent smell of the *Mercado Central*
the tiny Providencia markets
where we ate
baked corn pies   ate away
half-baked dreams of cross-cultural romance

Southern hemisphere
the other
end of the world
the soft light
the way his eyes avoided the truth

The full lips of the moon
the welcomed air at *Vina del Mar*
the freezing Pacific Ocean beach
on the first day of January
the meal at *Pomaire*

The workmates avoided
the sweaty smell of the airport
the fumes of smoky kisses
left behind
so many

airports   cars   private taxis
racing   churning
mashing
all that man
can accelerate.

THE DISAPPEARED OF CHILE

When I am close to the one I love
at least in geographical terms
I rejoice at the sound of my lover's gentle voice
but then he's off
like an airbus   flying out of Arturo Benitez

He has to work late   every night
he drives six hours
to his parents' house
in the luscious valley near Parral
where I am not allowed to visit

When we watch a film at home
his mother telephones
he goes on talking to her
as if he were cajoling
a secret lover

All soft purrs

whining murmurs

emotional blackmail   on both sides

half-hearted promises

they both know are hollow

No gold Dior wedding band here

he's certainly not the tall Greek of my dreams

there's nothing from Tiffany around my neck

except a figurative choker

of a Mapuche warrior.

THE PRINCESS MARY

I knew a Dane once blond of course
Peter Jens Nielsen so polite intelligent
I taught him English at least tried to

I should have frequented more bars
near sporting events athletes' villages
drank a little more like a fair dinkum Aussie

Mayte... *Oi, oi, oi*

I am now alone with my dying process
day to day dogged hours
my dog the notion of something bigger

I remember being touched
a man speaking the truth
the good the bad the ugly

I am not ready   don't have a will
burial or cremation   what a consumer's dilemma
we go to wars   but we want only other people's children to die

Embrace death   palliative experts advise
No, thank you   give me Paris   Prague   Peru
the smell of his hair   his cobalt eyes   his Latino hand.

EASTER ISLAND

Letting go isn't as difficult
As one might imagine
It registers haltingly
Like the fact they accept only US dollars
At the airport on the island of statuesque totems

But then   you move on
Take in the barren bereaved beauty
At last the plane arrives
Smoky schizophrenic Santiago
Finally the digital map shows *zero kilometres*

No more bag checks no X-rays
No more stamps in my passport
No more rubbery airline food
No loose useless foreign coins
No hope of new blinding love

I recall the endless maddening flights across the Pacific
The three bothersome hours of transit in seething Argentina
Then going back   the same way   on another smaller flight
Easy-peasy now   to fly direct   to the heart   of Chile
Straight to the heart   of the one you love   oh those eyes

If only there was more money
More hours at one's disposal
More chronological time   damn it
To hear your mellifluous voice speak
Dime que me quieres di nuevo

Before I fall at your feet
Asking you to gently explain
All those scattered eerie statues
Across the devastating landscape
Of your frozen Chilean heart.

THE ROAD TO NOWHERE

A week has disappeared in a dust-storm
like the roadrunner   your smell loiters
I miss the firm way your fingers envelop mine
snug   a false grip   I know can hurt more
than your consistent non-commitment
a softer texture to them, bony, briefly solicitous
evidently   you've lost some strength
a gun has misfired   a few years ago
you were a brute   like a rugby star
despite the definition of your acquired gym body

Niggling night thoughts unnerve me
I held you   like I used to
you sleep   pull apart
even in your sleep   if I lean in
too close   the bed is not wide
to contain the distances we both have travelled
singular, foreign lands we plan to explore
peeling away layers of languishing selves
for we are full-time long-term companions

Ineligible for IVF   in both of our countries
we shall remain barren of our own child
how can the self-loathing go away
when exclusion from normality is our reality?
My revelation stunned you
I brazenly admitted you would leave me
when I am gravely ill
you'd already be long-gone   if only
I could hold onto your luminous eyes
as I slave away   tending our imaginary lovechild.

AVENUES OF LAS CONDES

Driving in reflected threads of the Andes dimming sun
Smiling intermittently, vague like an old fumbling aunt
Infallible belief this is meant to be
Gently my head rests on your left shoulder
Your woollen jumper, your own smell intoxicating
Wrecking ball to my mantra   not to allow you
To affect me like a power surge.

SNOW DISSIPATING ON THE ANDES

Your lapis lazuli gold wedding band remains
    unadmired

Still I am hoping to disco dance once more
    dear friends

Dance Isaiah's holy dance in full theatrical regalia
    in a couture groom's suit

Several lugubrious days left   before I succumb
    a rapturous *paso doble*   a halted marriage

Naturalmente none of this matters to you now
    nor to me   trust is broken you see

You're still bald like you always were Mr Providencia
    Mr La Serena on the weekends

With that insipid blond pretending you were just friends
    I mustn't be bitter

There are none of Lorca's hysterical women locked here
desperate for a wedding night   a consummation

Only a visit to Neruda's empty house in groovy Bella Vista
a final *pisco* sour.

REPENT YOUR SINS

Abuse
A forced migration
A father removed from biology

A seismic D-minus in loving
A repertoire of foreign liaisons
A finicky fifth language to learn

A cumbersome bottle of duty-free Illva Disaronno
A self-certified virtuous man
A septicaemia virus   In a sauna in old Santiago

A city looming large   Skyscrapers   Street vendors
A fiasco furtively dating
A man in the throes of a break-up

A thwarted clandestine encounter in a cheap hotel
A rickety funicular in seaside Valparaiso
A return flight fully-ashamed and unchosen

A voluntary thrombosis
A name uttered in vain before surgery
A confused wake-up call in a recovery room

A pithy request for forgiveness   a decade later
A cold mathematician's explanation in rote-speak
A long while overcooked to be genuinely genteel.

DO YOU LOVE ME PLAYING AS SOUNDTRACK

Born within the ancient walls
Nicosia
Bombs fell
Premature but intact
Skin a little darker
Than expected

Older siblings
Usurped authority
Tried suffocating me
Mother admonished both
Disappointed
I was not a girl

Decades flow   A life filled with flotsam
Another Continent   Chanced
Across your path
Yourself transplanted from Falcone
An artist   I understood
But my Italian was rusty

Meeting where we did
We could not sing along
Nick Cave   playing
Muffling sounds in your empty flat
Mould filled the air
Yes, it's a great view over Centennial Park

I should have been more switched-on
Able to see through blatant lies
Read the tiny movements
On a face about to betray
Deviations are fair game
When you've been unwanted since birth.

THE ARROGANCE OF THE FRENCH

Thirteen Metro Lines
Countless station transfers underneath tunnels

Which take forever to negotiate when febrile
Is this truly Paris? Glorious *Paree*?

Tunnels furiously filled with fugitives
From unblessed places in the world

Fatigued *gendarmes* intercepting anyone
Appearing furtively illegal

Shrieks emanate from fleeing women
Dressed in all the colours of the rainbow

Thank goodness I'm not tanned this Spring
Filth at my feet is decidedly Third World

The French The real French The bourgeoisie
Who can easily afford stylish cars

Will be shocked to learn
What manner of criminality goes on underground

Beneath the bright boulevards of their City of Light
In Chile   A lifetime ago

Colleagues at the uni freaked out I used the Metro
My fall from grace instant   no sex scandal needed

C'est la meme chose in Gay Paree *j'imagine*
Wow! I can speak French fluently at last

I even helped an old lady from Lyons   She queried
If I were German   slapping down my multilingualism

In the evening in the Queen Mary hotel   Recovering
A breakdown induced by Camille Claudel's *The Waltz*

I counted the days since I had eaten a meal
My *baguettes* are discarded after two measly bites

Recidivist nausea   now a daily routine
Like my *pastourma* birthmark on the edge of my cheek

Yesterday his azure eyes   formerly from Tangiers
Now residing in a ghetto *banlieue*

Traced my history correctly in about three exchanges
Dime-moi he said in heavily-accented French

Have there been any spectacular sunsets
In your four decades?

PARIS EARLY SPRING

I counted twelve avenues
Heading off from the *Arc D'Triompbe*

Five languages plus the Cypriot dialect
Churning like whipped butter in my head

All the sugar-drenched fruit of residual guilt
Gorgeous little cars everywhere the likes of which

We don't have   Accelerate rally-like
A young woman   beautiful with little make-up

Driving a Citroen   In front of the *Pointe Neuf*
In a minor bingle   With a suited businessman

Elevated tensions   Over barely a scratch
My mother taught me the French had *charme*

Unbelievably   I am standing on Gallic terrain
My God!   There's the Eiffel Tower lit-up!

I am walking the genteel streets of the 16th *Arrondissement*
Where I've instructed my brother I wish to be scattered

So little *temps*
To visit all the magnificent museums

Set things right   Yield control
Write a will   Arrange a farewell

My life   A veritable symphony
A celebration   A confluence of experiences

Recalling   Walking up shoulder straight
Speaking French   Placing my order

With *Madame*   at *Dalloyau*
Fluent authority   on show.

EDMUND WHITE SHOULD BE AN OPTION

The first time I read Patrick White
I kept running to the dictionary
Frustrated by the preposterous set-ups
Olympic Gold Medal swirls of his diving words
Impenetrable, vociferous
A complete Classicist show off
Insufferable really
My tutor, who hated wogs
Gave me a distinction on my paper

Reading White in middle-age I surprise myself
Still need a thesaurus
But the shenanigans on the yellowing pages
Do not seem so theatrically surreal
Interacting with others is always fraught
Especially with the highly-strung amongst us
Our Noble winner's work an exaggerated documentary
Of the sorts to be offended without invitation
I bet my bronzed electrician is not *au fait* with such people.

STILL LIFE

And here is the famous coastline
The rapturous beaches he wanted to swim in
The tiny café filled with regional *wannabees*
Where he tried to have a bite to eat
Non me gusta

The surf shops he found enthralling
The menacing rocks we climbed
The vicious surf
Smashing us
The glass cabin atop the hill

He is now gone
Like all the handsome men I have cared for
You are the love of my life he said in his language
But he is no longer
Holding my hand

Only these luminous landscapes of our travels
The kitchen with its thick granite bench tops
The second WC he dribbled on laughingly
His spare shower gel
Left behind his luggage bulging full

His body-wash on the fastidious linen lasted two washes

The pair of boardies he forgot to pack in the laundry basket

The geraniums on the balcony floating

Down to the alley   Everywhere

A tableau of his soul intermingled with mine.

MELBOURNE TRAMS

The Europe of the South
glitters
storms
glistens
and shimmies

Its melting pot
delivers more than
unreliable paramours
flirting in its arty lanes
And the coffee? *Best-in-show.*

THE SMELL OF COFFEE IN ALBERT PARK

I am singing out loud like a madman
By the man-made lake near your rental
Gentrified cottages spruiking spring blossom
The smell of burnt coffee emanating
I am heady
Homeless

I am a Greek bearing gifts *sfogliatelle*
A simple vase for your Madonna lilies
My mother's preferred flowers in the Sixties
When she could afford to buy cut flowers
Before the war
Before her instant hysterectomy

Before her resolve vanished
Her modelling was dated like her hairdo
Her love all-consuming
Soul destroying
Mine is not dissimilar
No half-kernels of walnuts are wanted

The Italian crystal glasses clinking
My tote bag swishes too   is neutral
Butch like a heterosexual pop star
Like you   you sly Sicilian
You P. P. Pasolini of my darkest hell
Part-time lover of my supermarket days

A veritable tableau of bourgeois contentment
Fresh linen, a kiss in the cosy kitchen
dinner in preparatory disarray
You ask what music to blast and blare
Humid again   we concur
I censor my bullet train of words

Allow snippets to stop   at your station
Silence is golden so endless words are verboten
I aim to please
To be validated by your rationed force
my bored therapist could not bring you back
to this small table as a team   a family

I am singing with you   in unison
a song celebrated by bereaved lesbians
just three days united   in a home
Joy   like a magnolia tree in bloom
You are my life   my death
my complimentary drink at the open bar

The naked tree of our love will have no harvest
Only   our truth   will save us
The way we leaned   to hold each other
Those savage nights   of estrangement
We can sizzle steak   drink wine all we like
In the end   night will surely come.

THE LORD GIVETH

You buy terracotta lion book-ends I spot
In a spiritual shop burning incense on St Kilda Road
Sixteen degrees   late Winter   on a Sunday
I babysit your buys   you swiftly shove gears
Your Fiat 500   in a tram's nose
Burn rubber baby   I scream exalted   ashamed
We are playing house   so successfully

Synchronicity   six of your cronies
Coming out   of a café   immediately
Checking me out   a cow in Riyadh Market
I am overcome
I do not subscribe to glossy ghettoes
My target audience is not into disposable *play*
I am inconsequential   un-studly really

I whip them all
On their waxed behinds
My virility is intact
An earring apparently is still outré
None speak French
You boys have a great time
They sneer

There's that tv comedienne
Isn't that the girl from the soapie?
Is that who I think it is?
Tarot card readers
Cake shops and restaurants
Aspiring beautiful youth
Scrawled on scattered stools talking fame

It's glorious *amore*
Bastardo, maledetto, disgraziato
Love of my life, my husband, my wife
Brother, son, father and friend
Laugh for me some more
Shop for me snore for me
Consume me raw

Your olive skin holds me
Like a spoon holds thick fig jam
Fingers entwined without wedding bands
When you fall down the irretrievable latrine
Your *famiglia* will give me nothing
Mine will give you just a hiding
For wasting metered time.

WE SHALL BOTH BURN IN HELL

It is perfectly normal to need another, *non è vero*?
Someone you get along with   share a culture
Similar food, your music collections fraternal twins
A waitress asked me if we were brothers
I replied we were blood brothers actually
The result of a certain ceremony

On Chapel Road
I fell exultantly in love
With you   again
It was the way the neon lights picked up
An implacable silver hair
Your crew-cut black, matching my dreams, outsourced

My spirits lifted   sharing your quietude
Despite knowing the longhand words for I.C.U.
I suspect I shall die   alone
You'd be gone, long gone if I live a normal life
It is not pleasant, having such thoughts
But there goes the wind again, and this time

You pull your Mambo jacket tight around your new body
I am getting the results I've always wanted   you boast
You ooze virile charm sought after in backrooms
Those catacombs of poisoned instant lust
Unswept by virgin desire   untouched by grub
I am bleeding

Rebelling with unadulterated need
For your hand to touch the back of my neck
Your lips on my forehead   or anywhere
Our relationship a kinematic link
Rigid with fear
Until you discover my unwritten note

Asking for your honour
I am insatiable
Let me in
Let rip this darn lock, let me
Repent your urban sins
Confess your kerygma.

FOR GRACE RECEIVED

The question of unmet needs
perplexes men of a certain prototype
daily

cruising parks and cubicles
craving non-aligned fulfilment
wordless

any disconsolation left in their wake
is a side effect of no consequence
a non-event

non-entities those they use for convenience
bestowing upon them hollow Alpha male
affection   no beatitudes

the discarded   multiply daily
are forgotten   even a Christmas wish
a hello   is verboten

you exchange semen
yet are classified as strangers
it is bizarre

passive participants in these male rituals
usually shop for one
share unglamorous houses

single   on their birthdays
a celebration without a decent partner
no *per grazie ricevute* in the corner.

A STALE KISS FROM JUDAS

Can you breathe all right?
Is it because I decommissioned the six-pack?
The fact I am not hung like your spine-killer?
That I am a sexually demanding short man?

I hear your voice and the plight of Cyprus is not urgent
I kiss you on the cheeks   the gruesome weather shines
On the interminable tram   I am calm   wise
Soon your greeting   will taunt me in its surety

You do not love me   but you know
I love you to the moon   the stars   the galaxies
I'll inhale your smell from your clothes   after
I'll swim under the bed covers, breathing your scent

My father has not relinquished mum's clothes
Never   he claims   you and me?
There shall be no wedding   album
This is only an affair, no baptisms, no legal status

Only brevity, a razor at my throat when memory rewinds
Savouring conversations on Chapel, Collins, Southbank
Echoing other dialogues   in the heat in the small flat
In Centennial Park: it's been eons since I came so rapturously.

COMMUNION AT PRAHRAN MARKETS

Did you cube your onions
in that particular OCD way of yours tonight?
they shall be desecrated into the spit

the sizzle of your pan subsumed in oozing juices
the smell intoxicating   almost exotic
your foodstuffs carefully selected with a Sicilian eye

in the Prahran Market
pretending not to notice the starved glances
you covet   and earn

I walked silently   by your side
imagining   a resonant life
an obstinate child playing hide n' seek with death

Sex is not merely a matter of feeling good
it stops there, does no harm, only feels good
zip up, wipe your mouth, mime a pathetic smile, leave

continue rehearsing the scenes of your life
as divined by fate
nothing much more than an emission

Did you remember to throw in some broccoli?
it's good for cancer, my father eats it all the time
to heal himself.

I fill in the gaps with re-enactments
obliterating factual history
not even a red-bricked flat to declare our solidarity

only re-imaginings   your elongated silhouette
chopping, frying, stirring
tending me   till I'm done.

DOMESTIC DEMI-GODS

I am too avant-garde for IKEA
Our communication is wily enough in a look
Words extra cream on a double-shot iced coffee
Bacia me you ask gently
I do
E un altro
I do

I peel snow-peas   you tend your wok
It is peeling prematurely   like us
Perforating   soon to be landfill
All out of warranty
Putting together disassembled pieces of useful things
Yields bucket-loads of laughter
Admittedly after a few false starts, a swearword or two

Your body clams up with tension
You flinch from me   maintain a smile
It must be an ego boost having me here
I am not ugly   old men of the theatre harass me
only last week a Maltese angel held me
Smelling of youth, just twenty-two
shattering walls, sharing blood

Sibilating snoring ceases   starts in a sing-song
I a minor deity, a silenus, a leader of satyrs
Although not bald
We only have your obstinate love
A piercing glee in your laughing eyes
When you look at me you can't help but
Smile, admit it *signore*, you see the love.

NIGHT OMENS

Last night he kicked me again
His body parts dancing unexpectedly, in spasms
His accidental touch burning me

Like eggs frying on bitumen in summer

Tonight he woke up screaming in pain
His joints were piercing him in two
He will turn thirty-nine in January

If we get to his birthday

I held him whilst he cried
He did not acknowledge I was there
He was bungee jumping   planets away

All his muscles on his side, genetically on track.

MEASURING APOLLO

We're together again
Two and a half inches separate us
Segregate us in height from each other
In bed   the distance is just that
Down there   the same difference

Power walking on the beach at Apollo Bay
A Winter mist   *Is this heaven?*
He's two and half feet in front
His limbs elongated   sinewy
I remain swarthy   stumpy

I want to speak
Call out in competition with the swirls of surf
Hey, this is it! This is as good as it gets, buddy!
It doesn't get any better than this.
I've learned though   to shut the fuck up

The disquiet inside feels like surprised ecstasy
As I walk steady towards his back   towards
Remembering his arm around me   three am
The two and a half inches of space which divide us
As we drive around the majestic coast in a slick cabriolet

As we prepare dinner   narcissists   near each other
Two and a half inches   our breaths caress   as he asks
Do you ever think of mermaids? That someone beyond the horizon?
Those inches metamorphose into an un-crossable strait
Our song will always remain the same

Until life turns over the last unfriendly card
The laughing clown in colour   sadistic
Then six feet will replace those inches
Measured time and time again
Between us.

THE LETTER INFORMING ME HE IS DYING

Four times the maples trees have shed their glory
Compelling   silence   quietly separating us
Our exchanged   saliva   our DNA   binding us
Only the hiccup   of his call   out of the blue

Once a year   from unexpected ports
This year he requests an address
I want to write you a letter but don't know where to send it to
Perfectly encapsulating concisely the story of my life

Languid   weeks followed   life unravelled
Mum in intensive care   catatonic
An unsightly wound   wantonly open
A cow butchered in a backyard abattoir

He writes he was suicidal when we met, HIV diagnosis fresh
Gifting out gonorrhoea   by spooning me   both half-asleep
No sex that night   unusual   for lovers with dangly bits
Bits and pieces push, touch, brush by other bits   I guess

He took my love freely   spared me no foreplay
It's blatantly clear I'll never love you the way you love me
He said calmly   the night I wrapped my life in Australia
Helped me pack my fragile china in white tissue paper

An expert in how to gift-wrap life with no mess
He had impaled   shrivelled me   left me
Barren
A green   rock-hard fruit   birds   flew past

No escort to the airport, no love on the last night
Absent when I willed the plane down over the Alps
I flew into wishful greener pastures full of my type
Needing to graze   unsatiated   for decades

Truly   the letter   came long after we did
When it finally arrived
Greece condensed into three packs of photographs
Ioannis's sycophantic letters (I knew how to deconstruct)

The vista of the Acropolis from Nikos's apartment
Churning me like unsalted butter whisked with flour
I'd telephoned thirteen Melbourne residents bearing
His Sicilian surname   I knew   intrinsically

I was speaking to his deaf father   a genuine peasant
A man much like the father I knew
I understood he was in the *citta*   narrowing his geography
He often chose to whore himself   in exchange for board, rent

I was like a scorned mistress   a *putana*
Chasing after the only son
My stinging eyes (it's amazing how many men wish to humiliate)
In a big city men want to break you, superimpose their masculinity

So riddle solved: he is in his hometown
I've never spent Christmas with his family nor he with mine
Yet we investigated crevices and dark places
Fields of brilliant gold   dizzy   with male desire to be rich

Our fathers should have stayed in their Mafia villages
No water pipes no street-names no refrigerators
No surnames
SIMON is my father's first name   well it's ΣΥΜΕΩΝ

But try buying an omega   a monotonic point as a hat
Hell, a diphthong   at the port   in Limassol
When all mum cared about was to spare us
Limbs intact from dedicated bombs

Yes, we are different   as everyone is   yet fraternal
Stubborn for stubborn squared
Twenty-six years of institutionalised schooling   for me
Street smarts and cash-in-the-hand wily cheek   for him

Please don't let me die   before I see Red Square
Before I own a small dilapidated house by the sea
Before I've worn a Cartier wedding band
Vows exchanged   in solemn bucolic surrounds

Without Mum   Mum not knowing
Mum not singing like she used to
When she could smile her devastating smile
Beaming in a church   her graceful playground

But I digress
I am telling you aspects of my mother's story
I have no ownership of these
In him   I have a stake   a usurped right to tell

Tell me doctor
Is he on his skinny back   breathing
Man-manufactured breath
He was always so lithe   so slight

Will I get a shock when I see his open coffin?
Will I be allowed to claim a legitimate status?
Will anyone at his suburban funeral recognise me?
See the empty cavities carved in my heart?

Amore, Carissimo, Tesoro   I hold onto these   common words
Others more pornographic   all obliterated
When his eyes are closed   shut forever
Shat out   Imagine- not a single photograph together.

CAPE OF GOOD HOPE

Yiorgos and Maria
keep me company

Every morning at nine
Good morning, Greece

He his mother's pride
she a stylish sweetie

Advice they dish out each day
they're discussing drivers today

Yiorgos doing an O/B hands out
brioche and a red-blood egg

To the unshaven policeman who directs the traffic
the highways become killing fields during the holidays

Thanks a lot mate he tells him
recognising each other's entrenched masculinity

Yiorgos is going to the village this year
his family is roasting a lamb on a spit

To Mykonos Maria will cruise with all her entourage
at Syngrou I shall stay without a single drachma

I watch in envy   tremulous   because
everything that is good in the world reminds me of you

In a little bar on an island listening to Arleta
an Easter drink to toast absent lovers   those dead

Two or three shots with Maria the chatterbox
four or five cognacs with Yiorgos the good luck charm

Always impeccably-dressed the two of them
well-adjusted   carefully screened   selected

Both good-willed   well-disposed
worn shoes they shall never wear

Maria sometimes serious like an old schoolteacher
looks straight into the camera and quotes statistics

We've got to be careful guys
and thank God every day, okay?

Yiorgo   all man   flirts   like he should
he's always teasing Maria   a dinkum dude

Today she's thrilled Vidal Sassoon is doing her hair
Yiorgos still on the streets, giving good wishes to all

In my empty basement room I am staring at mould
shooing away mosquitoes which pester in celebration

I implore the screen to save me   the fickle one
unrequited   unrivalled   devotion   I send

But the hosts are not indefatigable
partners friends families homes   all

Await them with open arms   kisses   chocolate eggs
all the customs they maintain with strict adherence

So they belong to society untrammelled
I   unvarnished   unversed   remain

Wondering whether my decimation will renounce me
one blood-stained beautiful day

My hand will no longer be remaindered
holding my own Yiorgos/Maria in glee

A magic watercolour   our shadows
on the edge   of the bluish sea.

CLARITY IN HEROD ATTICUS STREET

The regime I'm documenting
At Constitution Square
One crisp early evening
Late Winter   Athens
The doctor   By my side
Well   That may be overstating it
City folk   Criss-cross by
The traffic   Utter bedlam
Since Karezi, Vouyiouklaki were stars

We had done some shopping   for his birthday
In a spotless exclusive shop   Marousi
The sales assistant as she took my Visa
Whispered hoarsely in faultless English
He's got the best bod!
My companion who'd passed Cambridge Proficiency
At fourteen no less   Had no idea
Caged as he was   In his hedonism
Gazing in the mirror   Irrefutable leniency

I serenade roses   in thirteen hues of choice
Buses boom by   Brutalising us both
Creating shadows   On our gloom
Bold   I buy five   Cream-coloured
The owner had travelled a lot   On ships
Showed great interest   In us
The doctor was silent   His mouth taut
With teething   He was glaring at me
As if I were a kernel   He bit into in a rush

Anger   Rage   Humiliation
A clarification   Of my criminality
I demand   Demons I prosecute
Preconceptions   I mangle
He knew what we were
He: oppressive   I: submerged
We stopped   At a park bench
In *Irodou Attikou*   I knew he did not wish to kiss me
We loved this street   Or did I just think that

What will I tell my mother
When she visits
Who shall I say gave them to me?

They're not red
It's not Valentine's Day
Why should you have to explain anyway?

You just don't get Greece
I don't?
Evidently not

Desolation unfolds   I was so close to perfection
Tears   Frustration   His finesse   Trussardi
Hermes   Armani   An obsolete joke now
Roses for fuck's sake   Cream like champagne
The reason for terminating
A heart-felt promise   Made by
A Greek kissing   The edge of his crucifix
A pledge alongside   Milva's soaring vocals
Lasting a mere   Thirty-three days.

THE APOSTLE'S BETRAYAL

I left for the islands
Riding flying dolphins in winter seas
Sipping tepid coffees in cheap hotels
Raped twice on the same weekend

One a policeman, the other anonymous
Neither the least interested in my brain
Told me to shut the fuck up
One spat at me kicked me

Said he'd do the same again
He knew my type he said with derision
I wondered if the translucent light
Scrawled my secrets in code onto the Love Hotel walls

Must give off a scent even in a foreign language
I wonder how you sensed my awe
Kneeling quietly under that tree
My desperate worship all wrong

My eight-year-old voice hoarse
Gurgling to make legitimate sounds
Syllables gobbled in a rapid disco song
Heard by no one

I have the key
It is not a Sudoku puzzle
I am an educated man
Impotent to assuage

Consumed with need   to grab a strong hand   to belong
To a man whose fingers are thicker   than my manhood
Challenge him   to hurt me   black and blue
Lead me through the locked gates.

ROOM WITH BALCONY AND SEA VIEWS

He insisted   Santorini   In Spring
Without the hordes   I was curious   About Kea

I'd made two aborted attempts   To impress
To tesselate in symmetry   Alas   I confess

Might be nice   Our first trip   Seeing renowned sunsets
The two of us   Riding donkeys   Creating memories

Up volcanic rocks   Engulfed in blue   Pullulating light
Making our cross   Orthodox trained   Thanking God

Don't leave me this way
Wailed a diva   On the Flying Dolphin

You fool   I thought
Haven't you learned that men don't think like that?

How you feel   They are blind to you
Once the decision is made   To move on

To erase you   You're now a naked tree
Never to bloom   Good only for firewood

Half-way up to the geranium-covered hotel
I unravelled

Perhaps it was all the trellised roses
All that radiance   The white-washed walls

The donkey was startled   Complained archly
I feared a beastly mutiny   A broken back to add

To my world bank   Of disabilities   My stoicism
Borrowed platelets   Inserted ever so slowly

Don't leave me this way...
A mantra   Chanted in an effort to carry on

The brutality   Of knowing you have an overdraft
On life   Long before seeing amaryllis

It was time   To sink into
Cycladic crisp waters   in May

Allowing the freezing Aegean waters
To desiccate the tumours

Sail me   Steadily
To a nameless islet   Seen in the distance.

RESIGNATION

this evening
three mouths constricted him
the other day
two others
but the pleasure was constipated
the evzone in the park
the parliamentarian in the parking lot
the teacher at the beach
three roosters crowed
the other two
who knows
Wolf! they cried

he didn't hear them
he didn't feel them

the Holy Triad
they were not
the notion had passed
a dispenser of love
he wasn't
he had disinherited it
totally

indignities had dispirited him
disjointedness he preferred
a screw   that needed tightening
three minutes max
and the job was done.

SON OF ZEUS

We met in a precious Byzantine church at Easter
The hymns, the incense, my trip to Mount Athos
My need   a man who ruled   beside me
His friend, all of twenty, glorious by his side
A congregation exalted on religious ice
A crucifixion so beautifully erotic it was sadistic

He fixed me with pinpoint exactitude
I made an excuse for fresher air
Roseate faces confronting my desires
I want you
I want you more
Porno stars look weird fully clothed

Three years   nine months
A courtship littered with love-letters in long hand
Cell phone convos costing a deposit for a luxury villa
He lost most of his dubious hair   he was now free
Marco was dead
I grew heavier   than he would have preferred

Christmas in Greece with my true love
My own demi-god whose feet I bathed
On our first night a cunning intention
No one sung *rembetika* in our empty tavern
I was prepared to make any sacrifice
Lost my way in a suburb straight out of disarray

Met an angel called Stefanos (*was* he an angel?)
My scruples were exorcised
No rosewater was needed for my special blessing
Orthodoxy can be interpreted in all sorts of devotion
My *mal entendu* maims me lame
I was trying too hard to find a supermarket

Liquid disinfectant placates me brutal elbow action
Bathroom brilliance I sought to reflect in pools of love
He greets the dog before me uses the WC dribbles
I should install you here as the cleaner
Were the kindest words uttered
By the face I imagined would be beatific

The outdated reel of my life projects scratchy frames
The trip to the bank   makes me recoil
I am a cash cow   There is no bread in this house
Muscle powers, liquid steroids, final notice bills
The dried sperm   on his clothes   is not my own
His only gift   a re-gifted book   on Greek Style

A request made I mustn't cry as this reminded him
Of his mother's tears for his absconded father
A shaky reassurance he shall pay me back
A lift to a down-at-heel hotel in Plaka
Look, we could still make it to Pilio, it would only cost...
And since we do not now need to order wedding bands...

I am abused   Not good enough   I have zero
Self-esteem   Viscera tumultuous   I do not wish
To hear any more   crap from any conceited male
I am forty-seven miserable years-old
Thought speaking the same language would help   heal me
In my mother country, birthplace of the entire Western civilisation.

SOME MEN

They were sitting in a *kafeneion*
the two friends the *pallikaria*
one perving on the girls mostly
at Kolonaki
the other entertaining soldiers
at Zappeion

They wanted to share
complex mysteries of the heart
but one of them was reluctant tonight
the other contemplating marriage
alone for many years now
they were the last to marry

They had travelled
had had a good time
had stayed out all night
many a time had cried
had dipped their toes
in all kinds of waters

And now
one of them got hitched up
with a younger woman
had bought a simple but gleaming ring
was afraid to tell his loving mate
who would never marry

So
they drank their bitter coffee
ordered another
and after
they went to their rooms
separate.

RAVINE

One of them was a Turk
The other a Greek-Cypriot
A national crime
Their relationship
In a country where both could be killed

Everything started all right thanks to lust
As it does always   Two men   Buddies
But soon enough   The Marbled King
The historical catalogue of injustices
Partitioned Aphrodite's Island

Constantinople or Istanbul
The disappeared of Cyprus   Religion
The fortitude of tradition   Disembowelled
Smyrna   Who would yield   Whose guilt
Was greater   Who   Would play the man

All these innate riddles
Discordant ingredients
A cacophonous disharmony
Like an unsightly irritation
An unidentified swelling

You're so bloody inflexible   one of them shouted
And you're so unbending   said the other
Dissimilarity
Disseminates
Liberalism

Later   Much later   At night   In their own greenhouse
Self-deprived   Of inherent rules of national history
Naked   Devout   Servants of demanding Gods
Understanding each other's basic needs
They map out   Their own culture.

PARADISE IS FULL OF SUPPORTING ROLES

The chill of the winds would sound
like a ship's constant horn
tossing sleep   even here   in a monastery
full of unshaven, unwashed men, high on precipitous ground
such utter peace   lust   solitude
a symphony of bells at five a.m.
a call to rise

Everyone in black
I was certain
I had already died
awaiting trial   retribution
excruciating pain
my sins miniscule   yet horrid
unforgivable

What good have you done?

To whom was your wasted love given?

The singing went on   unstoppable   monotonous
infuriating   cajoling me
sleep remained deprived   only
visions in kaleidoscope screening without censorship
urging me not to die   alone   but seek someone
a singing partner   to lead me
into the chorus.

POODLES IN BAVARIAN LAKES

He explained
It was the nature of men
To be hunters   Innate DNA
All men
When pushed

Normal marriages failed at alarming rates
Two men together   Less chance of longevity
He trusted his lovers implicitly
Would never cruise with intent
Placing him at risk

He was only window shopping
Sensing he had a philosophy to share
Like a voyeur?
Not really, just looking   To see if I still got it
Grab a man's attention in daylight

I'd been a diligent pupil
Learned only after a handful of lessons
If you look for trouble you'll find it
Easily in the world of men on the prowl
Solitude made me fearless of horny honesty

Prickly hunters dressed in recycled Versace
Chandelles having an apotheosis in Zappeion Park
Having buried several lovers   I felt nothing
Sole reliance on body rhythms   All of us
Like Amazonian marauding savages

We had brand clothes on
A signature scent costing over a hundred dollars
Expensive haircuts equal to a salary in some cities
We are Proust's disciples
Re-incarnated for our own diseased times

Spinning wheels of testosterone baggage
Tugging at our frontal lobe
Propelling us to action
We seal vulnerability in a vault
Cruising but not touching

Flesh
Is for the weak
Genuine macho hunters
Haul their prey
Home.

BARKING UP THE WRONG TREE

Serves me right
Thinking there was life after you
Somebody to love was possible
His voice sent shivers through me
My erotic fantasies propelled me
The word *hustler* also appeared briefly
Drawn in a rainbow on Neo-Classical arches
A brand new car (leased), unit (his granny's)
The job (he fucks his boss) the dog
A Newfoundland puppy pissing like a pony

Sommerville's funereal *If I could tell you* plays
We laughed as only two infatuated Leos can
I wince remembering we spoke of a wedding
An indefinite blessed future
Flights to Denmark for legality
We'd live in the Bay of Roses
Darkness lifted by an Athens Winter
Imagine   If I had shared more secrets
That whole entire last year was bliss
Truly I laughed so much my tummy hurt

The sacrilege of discarding pure affection
His tepid kisses spoke volumes
He sought a financial saviour
To extricate him from drudgery
This urban life came at a cost
A little puppy himself stuck in a flat
In Holargos, restless from monotony
My blind enthusiasm for the Motherland
Wavering like a half-erection
Light gliding me back to dried eucalypt.

THEOCRACY

I breathe residue of bushfires
You choke in scintillating Classical smog
Our extinguished love affair   limp
Suffering malocclusion   commits suicide
Somewhere in between
In the Atlantic Ocean

The incandescence of your rigid Greek maleness
Your pseudo-promises   a malediction
Fierce flagellation   a sadistic master
Going through the motions   a flippant chore

The decades of interaction have reduced me like a sauce
Bent over   not in a pew   my needs mute
The Lord's hymns sound muffled   pornographic
A heresy   in a language fading fast   from my lexicon

I assuage my guilt for worshipping maliferous souls
A tumescence so impressive it distracts from all else
I repent for kissing deities glimmering in fool's gold
An opalescence sending a jolt down my spineless being
Electrocuting skeletal memories of other betrayals
Eradicating demi-gods with a whiff of a wet dog.

MADONNA

Nobody told me
That each day
Would be like *Salo*

I was expecting to find
A companion who spoke my language
Not a circumcised Algerian extremist

Five times
A day he must wash
Pray

He tells lies incessantly
Kids himself that it is not egregious
Hence he'll be saved

He's a teetotaller too
But accepts he is a sex maniac
Veritable acrobatics condoned

It doesn't add up
I don't understand him
When he's on the telephone

Goodness knows what's talking about
If it's even legal
His cellular is habitually locked

He's never eaten a *koulouri*
Or *shiamisshi* or made a *flaouna*
Assumes *Charlotta* is a girl's name

Regards Cyprus
As only a holiday destination
For young Britons who like to drink excessively

Dreams of buying his mother
A big bright house
Without ever working full-time

I too would like to
Openly make my cross
I admit this

In written testimony
I'm not a great acrobat
Nor a fan of difficult liaisons.

I RECALL ONE CHRISTMAS

Close to the end
What does anyone have?
A few handwritten love letters
More and more difficult to decipher
With the passing of the years

Vistas   digital photographs
By the seaside   that island
Flights   soaring   closer
Ever closer to the setting sun
Over the snow of The Andes

Syrupy songs in various tongues
Twelve-year-old emails   texts
Residue   tired perfume   fatigue
An aria   sung in Italian   a soundtrack of life
Mother's tortured passing   voices of the dead

The missing link in father's love
Watching the clock on a Sunday eve
Two thirty-six past midnight   craving
Close to a premature death   yearning
Sleepless   reading   expired love notes

Pledges whose script is out-of-print
A lexicon stripped of currency
Words that shall wreak havoc
Break your collar bone lest you dive into them
Old fool   jump if you dare   from the balcony of need

Do you remember our love?
The slow-days before Christmas?
Cheated   choking   chucked   cloistered in
A three star hotel in sleazy Plaka
Hoping for a different ending (outside locals sung merrily)

The generous dividend to last a lifetime
After decades of no-interest-paid investments
The penultimate time I was kissed
A dark Chilean angel holds the record
Mellifluous   Meticulous   Megawatt smile

All I remember   Is your malevolence
Athens feels cold   To the exiled   The rejected
The shape of a hand   The black hair on a forearm
The way a man's eyes lose focus in a flash
If he no longer wants to kiss you

On the crumbling dais   Not even Bronze
I came to set the earth on fire
To enchant you   To be your charming companion
But you did not deem me a celebrated champion
I'm dusty now   Like ancient artefacts in the Metro.

NEXT OF KIN

There's something burdensome
about planning one's funeral
One went to pieces when one heard of his passing

said the Dame ballet dancer tremulously
ever so stagey
regarding Nureyev's death

I am up there with all the virgin suicides
blown to smithereens
all in the name of martyrdom

Your loved ones
should really do the planning
the meticulous execution

It's what he would have wanted
someone should say in tears
pseudo   hyper-real   or even digital

This was his favourite piece of music
His beloved Feraud sweater in vanilla
His gold lapis lazuli cross from Vitacura

No one shall ever know
the tick-tock
of my mind's murderous mess

Some people are buried with their cars
No, really, I have read about it   at the hospital
Proust got too philosophical for chemotherapy.

WOUND

I buy a cheese-pie
every Thursday and Friday
from Ariston in town
every shop I see
is selling shoes

I loiter
in Lekka Street
reminds me
of the back streets
of Old Nicosia

I turn left   right
WHERE ARE YOU YIANNI?
assistants without customers
it's only ten-thirty
avoiding streets with cars

I see doves on window-sills
shutters shut
inconsolable soldiers
masturbating
in the Star Cinema

A sullen little church
an old beggar woman
everyone seeking support
all hungry for an itchy scab
of dried blood.

LAST DAYS IN SWITZERLAND

As the diminishing days draw nearer
I pay homage to Rainer Maria Rilke
who died at my age

Our huggermugger lives echoing the *malentendu* of penury
urgent sole missions to unearth misplaced longed-for bibelots
affordable rooves over our overfed fat-as-a-pumpkin heads

Countries, regions, islands, or sandy deserts
all elusive viable options when chequebook choice has absconded
deserted you without a timid fleeting wave of a royal goodbye

When you can no longer look youthful bank managers
a coterie of old friends or ex-lovers of *temps perdu* in the eyes
you're almost done: spurned, slow cooked to purulent perfection.

THE POLITICS OF DYING

A dinner table	Triggers dreams
Left out overnight	Stomach usurped
A rancid aftertaste	Camouflage it
Blunt can opener	Misshapen ill-fitting
Tupperware lids	Spoiled strawberries
No amount of icing	Can disguise
All the philosophy	All the rhyming couplets
Of a poet Laureate	The six-pack
Of a world champion	Surfer
Turned to jelly	The kindness
The empathy	All the emotional intelligence
The symmetry	The face of Ms Venezuela
Volunteered efforts	For charity
The less blessed	The starving millions
Entire continents	Africa
Central America	Eastern Europe

Your neat grooming   Good hygiene
The school report cards
Exalting your intellect
The fact you wiped your arse   Properly

All inconsequential   It is simply
Somebody else's turn   To dance.

MY EXIT HOME

Views to die for   The realtor's ad bellowed
In some ways the lazuline vista was all that   and more

The D' Entrecasteaux Channel flat at Woodbridge Hill
Expanse of an Aegean blue   A white ferry swathing

Gliding to Bruny Island in full Winter sun
Carrying produce   Bucket list passengers

And probably loads of artisan cheese across
And back   If it hadn't sold at weekend markers

You've always had a thing for water
My older brother declared

Instantly I recall a mini-me island boy
Swimming out beyond the indigo buoys at Kerynia

On the precipice   Unfamiliar with the concept of fear
Pure terror   Came *plus tard*

The refugee camp   Its depraved dwellers
Arriving on Olympic   The land of killer sharks

His small Japanese car broken down
At Peppermint Bay

The view magnificent
Needed a stronger adjective

To fully translate the majesty   The aquamarine chilly waters
My brother not so taken   Settled on indigo

Are you not asphyxiated   My burning question
Memories offered no solace   Despite the seascape

The first time   I was dying
I did not   This had let everyone down

It no longer mattered   Translucence perhaps?
All siblings with baggage   Silent like our father

Resigned to our limited lot in life
Emotionally lonely   Distant

Managing a malaise   Trauma
Worse for those partnered

I settled on *Cerulean*   In homage
To Shirley Hazzard's observations of the Isle of Capri.

FROZEN

Beyond Higgledy-piggledy
Humble Home-baked
Artisan Growers markets
The Isle of Tasmania

There is only barren
Ice Sleet Sombre
Dark skies Turbulence
I plan my escape

Flinders Island King Island
Wild winds Cheese Beef brisket
Too close for visitors
Possibility of anguish extreme

Macquarie Island is an option
But I am no scientist
Know *niente* about passive penguins
Mating for life Or slippery seals.

LES CHOSES CHANGENT

July 11, 2015 Remembering Mother

A wise old saying in French
A zodiac horoscope, Saturn and Venus battling it out, again
A grieving middle-aged perennially single man
A dying companion dog, pissing everywhere
A rented 1940s house in the Mountains
A white picket fence
A neglected garden filled with loose red bricks
A carcass of leaves
A long-awaited reunion
A lover who never quite materialises
A childhood secret not revealed to siblings still impacting daily
A Cartier wedding band in the three colours
A desperate act of amity posted to Spain
A spanking new will requesting no service- just
A luxury-grade padded coffin.

ORTHODOX

We were at the barren cemetery
no movie stars are resting here
working stiffs

immigrants with peculiar names
of all ages creed religion colour
her grave   wretched

somebody unknown
had placed gaudy plastic flowers
my father

riddled with two kinds of cancer
stared   assuredly   fragile
at his final resting place

his mouth taut
my own fear on hold
he silent

his unkempt eyebrows
a tactical manifestation he was living
his deep lifelines pronounced

in the midday Adelaide sun
his words   to her
were brief   to me   terse

what a mess
this business
of having to die

this business
of having to live
only to then die

knowing
you will be entombed
plot 137

this business
of loving someone
completely dead

I said not much
having just buried
my own lover.

ABUSE

I remember
sometimes
that I believed
in You
a sweet little angel
I was
singing
in your blessed house

now I always
fear my faith
since I'm losing it
running around on my knees
loathsome

each time
I am given a NO
clouts and punches (*pix lax*)
blood I swallow
trying to recall
YOUR song
a rag of self
to salvage.

TRACING HISTORY ON AN ISLAND FAR FROM YOUR DESERT

The days seemed shorter
awaiting your arrival
Mother would make such a fuss
dusting   cooking   polishing marble floors
ironing   till we all looked like Russian dolls
plumb with clothes

Your relatives would arrive
days ahead
throwing us out of our beds
it wasn't unusual to sleep across the bed
four or five of us
feet sticking out

Cousin T. showing off
his muscles   his privates
unmarried aunts snoring   like trucks
my sister glad to have female company
albeit from the villages
Mother was always a handful

The bath would be filled with ice
Coca Cola, Fanta, Seven-up
grown-up drinks spirits too
food had been cooked
by your sisters who believed
city folk simply could not cook

A twenty-something first cousin
beaming in his new Volvo
would act as chauffeur
(I preferred Geromilos's old tiny Triumph)
or was it Geromilos himself
I liked best?

Mother would make an occasion
out of the drive to the airport
threw coins into the new car
making us all laugh with her traditions
stopping for gelato at Makedonitissa
popping in to see her side of the family

Living in discreet affluence
salubrious tree-lined avenues
where no children were sighted
playing
perhaps to assert her own superiority
over the busloads of villagers

Then we would wait
for the plane
to touch down
your big sister would scream
she was always the dramatic one
(twice divorced before The Beatles)

You'd rough our hair with your huge hands
Mother would straighten it all back at once
no questions were asked of us
just quietude
obfuscated hints
of gifts brought back

In two weeks
you would be gone
leaving behind a smell of sweat
a debris of maleness
raised voices
Mother in constant sniffles

A day in the park
buying us ION chocolates
Sokofreta from the kiosk
a block each
and soon
soon

Your
blue
eyes
already
out of focus
in our memory

a letter would arrive
stamped with Arabic writing
a precious stamp we fought over
requesting us to send
our traced palms
on the thinnest of aerogramme paper.

DANGLING DICE

my father
who may not be my father
after all (stem cell tests)
is forty years older than me

my mother
who is dead eight years now
was thirty years older than me
until she died gruesomely

my son
if he were to be born
this year
would be forty years younger than me

my illness
is only fourteen months old
looks like a winner
wiping away my predicted life expectancy

by at least thirty-five years - *the best years of your life!*

my resilience
is yielding to steroid intake
which takes four hours to infuse
bloating me as if I had already died

my foul-smelling body
shall take ninety minutes to dissipate
into cinders   into shards
weighing just under three kilos   on average

all this arithmetic
seems so fixed
against my incompleteness
my lifetime's search for comforting.

MOVING IN WITH FATHER AS A MIDDLE-AGED MAN

The tri-level townhouse packed-up
Spotless   Possessions already in a container

The splendid emptiness
Could not be shared

The dog freshly shorn   trembling
Days he had been despondent

Not wanting to play
Pissing on the floor

He buried his snout into my armpit
On the way to the airport

Animals are attuned to mood
Some of us can't achieve orgasm in company

On the plane   The night definite   City remote
A foreign airport   Parked unlit planes   lonely

The stewardess not a fan of Botox
Kind of sassy   Motherly

I am grateful

She is looking after me

Tonight I need someone experienced

In the vagaries of life

To take care of me

I can hear him wailing below

Earlier on land

I embarrassed my brother

Clearly not amused

My indiscreet outburst about failure

Family can only cope

If I am in absolute control

Resilient Misfortunes

Resonating like jangly jelly beans

Forget the cancer

Fearful years of waiting for death

Unspoken

Transcontinental rejections

Failed careers

Naked dedicated toil

The fact I cannot afford to live

In the city I loved these four decades

I'm a has-been

Forlorn   Forgotten

In Paris

On my oncologist's advice

To live out my last wishes

Managed to meet an Algerian agitator

I want to leave this

Contaminated Ithaca

Morph into a new version

Taller   voice huskier still

Indisputably male

I wish to be more overtly masculine

Take firm adult decisions

Occupy emotional-free zones

Not pack my entire life

Seventy boxes the same size

Old work files packed

Faded newspaper clippings

Some cassettes even

Global telephone adapters

A torch

Possibilities

Let me lean instead on

Muscular rugby shoulders

Listen to me

Willingly

Without sending a text
Swiping right to meet a wired stranger

My kind of Alpha male
Would need to know

Intrinsically
A sprinkle of coriander

Served on a Limoges plate
Goes a long way.

FAMILY LUNCH INTERSTATE

I'm just so not ready for this
Bored already
Dismissive
My brother is exasperated
After spending mere minutes listening
To the old man
Raving in a stream of vaguely inter-connected threads

Conversation is all one has left
When the body is weary   not functioning
Unable to get an erection
Discarded in a lolly wrapper of humiliation
Kissed last   Decades ago
I'd understand it if our roles were exchanged
He has not seen his father in years

His litmus test lasts eleven minutes exactly
Lunch punctuating the effort to feign interest
Fine china   Wine glasses full   Home cooking
Should have provided sufficient distraction
We could at least pretend
To infer each other's bullet points
Maybe I'm just a lousy cook

You're becoming more and more like Mum
He says thinking he is being droll
I'm not laughing, pet
Being unpaid carer for a man in his late eighties
Is not my ideal last romance
Especially since the genetic doubt was signalled
Medical tests can paint such potent pictures

Present clarity of what is inside of us
An internal familial trolley
Which keeps veering
To the left
No matter
Which way
We seek to steer.

VITAL LIE

It was an old Thanasis Vengos/Taiyeti film that got me going
One of my dead mother's fuzzy videos
Absolutely no connection with my daily detritus
Except for the banal colloquial language

The topic was marriage, children, happiness
Subjects well-known at our breakfast table
Littered with black, anorexic olives, salty halloumi
Melon, Greek short-wave, black bitter coffee

The movie left me bereaved
Like a living livid widow
Cast aside for a svelte, youthful model
The other day I discovered a grey pubic hair

Scorned jokes came at a rate of one per line
Delivered in that 1960s shouted, over-the-top way
How times change when the dictators have gone
All they make these days are obscure titles
        tightly-clenched jaws
For superstars you'll have to go elsewhere   FILOPIMIN FINOS FILM
        has ceased production

I too have shut down
An Ibsen character
Waiting
To be called on stage
Waiting
To be heard
Seeking a forehead
A soft kiss
To bless.

THE DECENCY OF GREGORY PECK

Jack   Not Jackson or Jake or Jacob or the Jewish version
To him   I am the gay Mrs Kravits of the neighbourhood

Writing letters to the local council to investigate
A barking dog   Lest its owner is deceased

Collecting for the Red Cross, Smith Family
Medecins Sans Frontieres   Selflessly

Handing out savoury pastries I have baked
Loved the cheese thingo but there were sesame seeds

EVERYWHERE he revealed sheepishly
My, those perfectly aligned teeth

After Easter Sunday
The Julian calendar steadfastly observed

I was feeling reconciled   in a purist way
He encapsulates all the qualities of men

I have loved
Except for the foreign bit

He is decidedly Anglo-Celt
He is of this land

Well
At least from the affluent luminous suburbs

If I analyse his accent forensically
Sometimes his turn of phrase

Evidently is queer
I do proclaim a vague interest in linguistics

His hand movements too
The rolled eyes displaying

Dismay To be fair
He is a food stylist after all

He shows concern for me
As I stumble around the block

No

I'm certainly not drunk, thank you very much

Just drowning in chemicals infused intravenously

With my unequivocal written concern.

MY CANCER TASTES LIKE A FRESITA

Try a little of our sparkling Chilean wine, it tastes like strawberries
the nineteen-year-old liquor store assistant offers
I break out all in a sweat, my face wet
the teen looks away, ignores me
it is too hard for this generation
to deal with anything
but cyber emotions
emojis

I sit on a bench just outside
thinking of a train journey I once took
from Athens to Salonica   alone
tremors of beauty stirred   at every turn
swarthy moustaches   beards of soldiers
farmers' adult sons   sitting so close to me
I could smell the way they made love
or cried   lied   defeated

We cry a lot   us Greeks
it is innate   you can't avoid it
Have you heard our tragic songs?
No uplifting Evangelical gospel verses
No incomprehensible hymn
No Chilean folk song
could be so melancholic
surely

Perhaps I should have tried some sparkly
drunk a toast to the fallen men
in my diaries
to the man
who rules my blocked heart
make a wish
to getting rid of this illness
creeping slowly within my nodes

Trust me
not to acquire a fashionable disease
I blame my mother
like no genuine Mediterranean son should
She drank too much full-strength Coca-Cola
Ate way too much *pastourma* when pregnant
explaining the birthmark on my left cheek
my tendency

To simply buy a six-pack
instead of displaying one
I am not complaining   my love
I know you (don't)   love me
just the way I am
simply   God makes us
in the guise he wishes us to be
a priest advised me once   before kissing me

Singers dedicate traditional verses
broadcasting through my car
I am bombarded by pledges
hollow promises
pathetic Greek pop song lyrics
in the end can't bring any significance
into an average life
nor have any impact whatsoever

What then?
You are just a youngish
very sick man driving
his memories in a platinum silver car
the smell of pungent leather the only comfort
the only dubious certainty
in the hazardous road map
to annihilation.

LAST PRAYER

Forgive me father for what I have not become
As a grown man the son you had hoped for
Was it a pre-emptive hint that you left us all
Just when I turned two?

Had you chewed some predictive bay leaf
Seeing decades forth into the bleak future
True to your ethnic heritage
Renouncing weakness like the Spartans?

I recall a hunting trip where you shouted at me
Humiliating me with the final quack of the dead duck
Its still warm blood running down my leg
Whilst we sat in a borrowed beat-up heap of shit

All my schoolmates knew you did not live with us
You did not own your own car
Teased me you weren't my real father
Your sky-blue eyes on another familial planet

Forgive me
For not fathering the smiling grandchildren
You crave
For being part of the gig generation in work

For not being a gambling man
For keeping my inherited sperm to myself
(Well, that's a lie - I am paying them to freeze it).
God knows what else I have to apologise for?

Forgive me but it would be of great assistance
In this cavalcade of unearthed emotions
If you were to reveal the bungled tragedies
Inside the travelled corridors of your own mind

Your own inadequacies your imperfections
My older brother is reading *The Narcissistic Family*
He too irrevocably injured by your absence
"What is this word *affection?"* you famously asked last Easter

Forgiveness Father
Is something an Orthodox monk sought
Like an ice maniac on prescribed steroids
The monastery had depleted his foreplay skills

All he could do afterwards was mumble
A rote prayer
In the name of the Father...
You weren't ever there to protect me

You never taught me stuff how to play soccer
Shoot a goal Defend my own personal space
Show me how Be that square-jawed macho man
My good looks only invited harassment from older men

My relationship with you A constant fortification
Was the most non-spiritual encounter
On the amassed calendar of unsatisfying conquests
All simply savoured In your missing honour.

DANCING IN THE CITY

In the late 1980s   There were twenty of us
Some of us very pretty   Some ambidextrous   Ambivalent
Others a bit pudgy   Trying our best   Picking up
Lying too   If needed   About our status
About owning our own house
Driving a Beamer cabrio   It got some in

There was Donkey-Dick Dudley
Dominic, three Johns, a Darren, a Davo... a handful
Of fag hags   Albeit they never saw much action
Others whose names elude   And OMG!: *Amadore*
Simply saying his name made me come
Back for more   And more punishment

His blue eyes challenged the glory of lapis lazuli
I recall watching the Mardi Gras parade on a rooftop
More make-up per square inch than a Napoleon Perdis shop
Versace, Armani, Valentino would have been jointly horrified
The jarring home-sewn dresses of the part-time drag queens
All I wanted was to desperately hold his hand

I had been an altar boy
So I gravitated towards a chaste kind of love
Forever *The Tragic Greek*
To my more promiscuous Anglo mates
I was a late bloomer at twenty-six
Amadore had more aggravated visceral ideas

Dudley, who never understood the Madonna/Whore complex
Maternal-fed romanticism afflicting Mediterranean sons
(The object of your desire must appear to be pure as a virgin)
Crushingly told me straight-faced my unrequited leading man
Spent the previous night at *The Den* getting fisted
By a bearded bear with a beer gut wearing a Dorothy outfit

Sober   On the surface   I rejected the idea as supposition
I had been led astray by novels I read for my Honours Year
Southern European men spelled trouble, spoilt by their mums
Amadore was a complete narcissist   long before *Seinfeld*
Made it a thing   He could not string two words together
Except *Fuck me!*

Years went by   speedy as a Summer storm
Two decades   The music stopped
Everyone it seemed   Had died
Everyone we remembered dancing all night
I was diagnosed with terminal cancer
Had no one to call   To share this with

I heard Dudley was miraculously still alive
He was fond of cruising nude beaches
Perpetually had his size-queen fans fawning
He was a rural heir of some kind   Farmland?
He never divulged such things only freely broadcast
His tantalising tackle to complete strangers

I only mention Dudley   As I bumped into him
A day before I started my last round of chemo
He admonished me for having aged
He was still a *Gonna Wanna Shoulda Woulda* sort
Espousing tabloid pseudo New-Age recycled theories
To the best of my knowledge he'd never held a paying job

Holding on to my dead mother's words
If you have nothing to say, don't...
I averted eye-contact   Taking in the naked flesh on display
Shaved pierced Prince Alberts   waxed, bulging, droopy
My god? What in hell was *THAT*?
I was hallucinating on masses of prednisone steroids

Geez you've piled on the kilos, look at your gut!
Dudley was always brutal   Perpetually clueless
I did not retaliate   Mention my unfashionable illness
That night   I celebrated the smithereens of my youth
Martha Wash, Sylvester were spun Taking me to heaven
A sole sing-along   A bit of a dance

Admittedly not at the cruisy sweaty Hordern Pavilion
No ecstasy on offer   Only a cheap prosecco
In this dive   My treehouse home
Life partners all now dead   Thankfully
No exorbitant entry ticket necessary   A lie-down
On clean sheets after a couple of Paris Grey songs.

TEN MONTHS FROM HIS DEATH

12/11/2013

He is irascible   in private   filled with fear
Gregariously jolly in public   not letting on
He procrastinates
Even to make a call in his dialect

His cataract surgery   recovery is dragging on
He pisses onto the back seat of the toilet
Unaware   I sit
On a pond of stale urine daily

Has taken to sitting all day no television, radio on
Everything including the front door lock
Needs changing
Rusted, broken dusty or, just

Past its use-by-date.
I ponder   I flagellate
The machinations of his mind's bacilli
Easier becoming an instant lottery millionaire

I use the bedewed garden as a safe space zone
As inane conversation about meals
My several siblings   all absent
This stings us   both

These final days can be enjoyed
I insist   Challenging
My dutiful self
To reach a higher ground.

THE FLIGHT TO AN END

19/09/2014

The first officer's name was Santiago
he had an undercut then swirling layers
crimped into a semi-bouffant
no way did he wake up with those swirls

He had a touch of the-Ricky-Martins about him
facial features though not as pop-star pretty
acne scars showed when clouds blocked the light
my first thought: Chilean with a touch of Mapuche

As he was only 5 foot 4
just under thirty   at a guess
already with slight love handles
embellishing his belted waistline

I wanted very much   desperately
to imagine him   completely naked
that would demonstrate I didn't care anymore
but for some reason   I could not fantasise

It had been a decade   a dim dull decade
since I'd seen a man naked   like a satyr
since I'd walked the verdant avenues of Providencia
alone as that was the condition of my banishment

Why on earth did my dim-witted diminished brain
churn like a crazy blender mashing a hotpot of soup
obliterating all components until none were seen entire
switch the darn thing off   I need clarity to remember

I have not been blessed with gregarious smiles
I have disappointed everyone I have met
my ailing father   most of all
it is in his scowl, scrawled on his lined forehead.

GHOSTS OF WOOD SMOKE AND ASH

Banal words
On the mobile
Older brother is efficient
Bumptious even   Like a petty official
No rehearsal or first read-through
To prepare me
For this tragic multi-act theatre
He is a willing conspirator with my sister

Our relationship strained
Faded sense of sibling duty
Resolute
Righteousness
An electrical impulse
Shivers down my back

The epicentre
My sister's house
I am grudgingly welcomed
We fell out   Comprehensibly
Over dad
His exit care
A last-minute hotel in a laneway in Adelaide
In the southern dingy end of the CBD

The Central Markets closed
I walk to Coles Ostensibly
To buy fresh raw sustenance
I can afford Settle on
A shimmering pack of Kettle Chilli Chips
Local honey-comb chocolate from Macclesfield

Dressing his dead body
Freakiest show
Of my solipsistic life
Silent recriminations
Vehement vendettas
Adult nephews Niece
Agog at raw emotion
My image smashed

The chapel has a high ceiling
Scintillating stained glass
The male funeral assistant kind
He looked much smaller
Slimmer
A sandy sallow pallor

The forensic investigator in me
Convinced his organs were harvested
I sob   No masculine modesty
A soufflé of anguish   adrenaline
Ad alta voce
The young obese priest sings
His dirge in two languages
I'd stayed strong   For days

Middle-aged ailments
Mount my body
Maniacal rebel's revenge mission
Am I having a stroke
Have I died too
Is it my turn next

Blood pressure high
I should exercise more
Eat less
Was it yesterday
We buried him
In Centennial Cemetery
Or is it tomorrow
I am out of sorts

I see him In a narrow
Cheap unpadded casket
Waxy cheeks shaven
I fire an egregious
Shot at my brother
In that cried-out funeral home

A déclassé resting bed
Is it tomorrow
Or late tonight
We shall argue
Di nuevo
About an open coffin
Staunch Orthodox friends
Need to say a final

Feeble goodbye *Vale*
Farewell Face-to-face
Orthodox Tradition
Insists on our observance
Generations have done so
Discombobulated

Bewildered We cannot concur
Ashamed I was a spectacle
In church Shaming three generations
Strangers Grateful they still live
This is mad A folly
Unforgiving Surreal
Hysterical *A grown man*
His absence Literal

Palpable
Susurrating on every inch
Of the marble flooring
To the end
He chose obfuscation
Stubborn silence

Refusing a paternity test
Where is the salvation
The expiation
The spiritual mentor
A graceful God
To appease
Damn it!
Could someone get me a stiff drink?

Where is the long-sought *simpatico*
Lover to offer a strong arm
To rub belladonna
On my joints
He's delayed by a planetary transit
Perpetually lined up at the lost luggage desk

I crave sleep
Deranged Disengaged
Disempowered
Seek a stoic
Mellifluous voice
Cadences that soothe
This is a gore fest
Out-of-control

An Easter Show ride
Churning out scenes
From our pockmarked past
Pecking at us
Has he miraculously gone now
To a better place

An apotheosis full of fig trees
As the morbidly-obese boy-priest
Declared in inane false phrases
Is this mid-Spring storm rotting his casket
Do earthworms nibble
Ravenous rats gnaw
At his elegantly-attired remains
He abandoned us

That's all there is to it
Even in physical approximation
His plan was to time-travel
Elsewhere
As quickly
As a thrilling fully-throttled

Bugatti roadster
On an empty motorway
Am I flying
Driving on the freeway
To get home
Two and a half hours
From the city's airport
It is not the same airport

In the last divided capital
We waited for him
Waited And waited
Year after year
For him To come home
From the scarfed titillation

The far Middle East
A man bearing gifts
Hitchcock would turn this macabre script
Into a fascinating scenario
Unspoken Seething perversion
A mysterious ice-blonde the star
He was compliant in death
Offering each limb

To be dressed
With relative ease
His Valentino loafers
Hand-me-downs from me
In the corner
Sodden bloodied clothes

Packed nonchalantly by an orderly
When they discharged him
To die   Discarded now
Inside the narrow coffin
Oh the exasperating revulsion
Have I sufficiently handled dutifully
These ultimate symbols
Of our connectedness

Pointilliste landscape tonight
Serenaded by mutinous Mountains fog
I dread stepping on a brown snake
An enormous black spider
A creature more horrid
Approaching my rented house

Dead Gothic quiet
A ventriloquist's stored dummy
My elderly secretive neighbour
Panicked   In eerie darkness
Got herself locked out
Close to midnight
The day we buried him
It is done now

It is written now
A temporary makeshift cross
In another State
In his adoptive country
Saunter inside the vestibule
Slide on a rubber toy

Curse the Universe
Aggrieved, the dog
Engaged in roulades
Trills
A growl
Despair worthy of La Scala
And we are
One.

SIMMER

Filtered unrequested fury
Piffled pavlova on polished parquet
Alcohol withdrawal
Lack of friends at the funeral
The film I bought
In a cool shop where I was old
A sexless grandpa
Longing for a succubus

I solicited it for lust
A fleeting lascivious perve
Leading man with luminescent eyes
Dwindling bank account
Hosting my nephew
Melancholic already
Not yet thirty
I cannot save him

Culinary delights
No salvation
No preppy tantalising *muchacho*
Has planted a bay leaf bush
Just books other people do not buy
Au fait in many foreign languages
Middle-age angst ample
Calcified libido

Overfed
Disappointments aplenty
Desire diminishing
Stone dead
A yeast-less sourdough
High-potassium-magnesium-calcium
No sodium meal
Leaves me tetchy

The dog vomited yellow liquid
Remnants of the lamb shoulder
In the centre of the new rug I bought
For the upcoming inspections
Matching the bedside lamps

Collocating the bespoke light-fitting
Delivered by a dishevelled designer
Eastern European   At a guess

A hefty French vintage hardcover
Whacks me in its free-fall
The Eighties, Nineties and Noughties
Done   Dusted   Dusty
Decapitates one of the matching lamps
Bought merely a month ago now discontinued
I must downsize further
My fiscal multiplication figures demand it

My four decades
In the deep-freeze
Spotlight of lay-by fame
In the headlights of futile
Creative endeavours
Like *tapas*   Fleeting
A labyrinth   A brazen
Small sanctimonious country

Shall never allow it

Expiation rationed

Reserved

For sports stars

The mansions   The WAGS

Television screen time

Media press   Public adulation

Who gives a fuck about your book?

CACTUS

On my grave the headstone shall read

He tried
He tried hard
He tried real hard
He did try

He was a try hard
He tried it all
He tried too hard
He should have stopped trying

He didn't try hard enough
He was tiring
He got tired
He exhausted us all

He was tiresome
He should have learned to be more retiring
He should have retired earlier

He was all-tried out

He faced too many trials

He was a trial

He didn't even make the trials

Thank God for cremation

LASCIVIOUS

I am a rich man hiccupped by a poor man's history
Deplorable to stomach
Gazumped by a winning absence
Of income   of jubilant love   of legitimacy

In quietness, in confidence shall be your strength, Isaiah said
But the roads we solemnly travel are incomparable
Strewn with hedges that tear at your unsuspecting city-boy skin
A torrent of wind lashing you this way and that, interminably

There's a photograph from my high school dance
I am a veritable, feverish teenage dancing queen
Swathed in white silk pantaloons with bell bottoms as wide
Already being bullied by the older boys as a *flamin' poof.*

PRICK

What is it with poets and cancer?
All seem to be dropping off like the proverbial flies

At least their work remains
Slim volumes   A royalty payment of sixty-six dollars

For some lucky enough to have been published
Approved by the gatekeepers of *culcha* in *Ostraya*

The others   Without a copyright annuity in lieu
Oh these others

Twisted souls   Working in call centres, libraries, schools
In their own heart are considered major talents

Who is there to draft an obituary (not) for newspapers
Only a distant nephew shall peruse   briefly

From an insider's view   It all seems so grim
I know for a fact being dexterous with words

Gets you nowhere in your head-on with the Big C
Pronounced masculine veins on the other hand

Will make your battle a lot more dignified

Nurses will descend on you

Underfed wasps armed with needles

You're a poet with *girly* veins?

Nah, not so much

Creative types like that are simply hard work.

SELF-PRESERVATION AT HIGH ALTITUDE

This, my second Winter   Has shown me
I can distinguish the burning wood, the various kinds
Wood the local folk choose to burn at 1065 feet
This early morn, the ambience is of a honey-infused banquet
Don't ask for specificity - all I know is, it's not organic Manuka

I walk rugged icy paths with the wool dog as my god
Helios illuminates   All that is good   All that is horrible
This, my adopted world   All of us touched by something
Take your pick: age, cancer, depression, penury, co-dependence
Senility, abuse, loneliness, resigned desolation, all up for the taking

Fires, burning day, night, two hundred bucks of ironbark a truckload
Delivered: it burns slower, for much longer, the young man advised
Enormous blue eyes, six foot three, a silver thick wedding band
A smile that I couldn't quite interpret
Laughing at an aging fussy fag or bravado flirting?

My personal history has neutered me
From successful approximate interpretations of younger men
Best to avoid all interaction, it'd only lead to more nihilistic angst
I wish for no more heartache   Only a fire burning, in two quiet rooms
Endowing me discreetly with the primal machismo confidence I lack.

SUNDAY NIGHT ROAST

Pull your pants up!
Twenty-eight and can't pull his pants up properly
It would help if he had a semblance of an arse

Pluck that two-inch hair
Protruding like an obscene sin from your ear
I can't concentrate on the period piece

Tuck that shirt in for crying out loud
You look ridiculous in your forties
What kind of grown man wears an earring now?

Oh, here we go with inner-city, gin-infused leftist crap
The West is evil, complicit in others' misfortunes
Yet we all gravitate to it and insist on staying

Oh what a total wanker!
Superannuated on public service beatitudes
Give it a rest, what toss you talk

Here he comes- the host
That's the best they could find
In the whole of our vast country?

AFTER

Instead of getting rotten blind drunk
Like most would
Have at least three glasses of wine the nurse said

I sat down On the big day of remission
Making a list of all the words I could use
Post cancer

Tossing with Post-Modernism's take on illness
Illness as metaphor Sontag surmised
Post-traumatic stress_ take your pick:

Childhood sexual abuse, abandonment by father, a coup,
bombing raids, all-out war, rape victim, displacement,
Greek-speaking immigrant to the sunburnt country

To some in the world who do not pay attention
To anything other than money Additionally
I'm a failed: actor, writer, lover, son, friend

Film-maker, speaker of phonemic-perfect French, Italian, Spanish
Greek that hiccups fighting for dominance over my Cypriot dialect
English that hesitates with the roundness of the Queen's vowels

An assortment of visual images   Is all that remains
Post offices in Rome   Tetchy unshaven assistants
Correos in Chile   Where I took refuge in writing postcards

Nobody writes postcards like you
My former friend Dom exclaimed   Half admonishing me
Half praising   My intimacy with words

Post opening nights of my plays in theatre foyers
Post break-up with a bodysurfer boyfriend on his bike
We had to pretend to his mates I was his acting teacher

Post the cliché trolley-dolly
He had sequestered lovers in each corner of the world
His waxed back on display   in deceit of his real age

He stormed the Green Room riling the lesbian SM
Shouting at her: *Don't you know who I am?*
Her priceless reply: *No*

Post-operative care   Lost count how many times
No one to help   A cup of tea
Post walking the rambunctious poodle twice daily

Post the endless wretched hours on treatment days
Post parcels posted to J. lost in transit
Somewhere between the Adelaide Hills and Valencia

Post new Millennium Y2K ennui
Post Sydney Olympics   All the drug cheats
The hounded French runner made to flee

Post my first chemotherapy session
Bald like a newborn baby
And I mean EVERYWHERE

Post caring if I drove a 3.2 litre Alfa Brera
Post giving up on reciprocated love and electrifying sex
Post focussing solely on careers and moneyed success

A post scriptum
If I'm lucky to be included
On a little-read academic research paper

Commemorating minor poets
Independent Australian theatre
Between the years 1984-2024.

SWIMMING IN WORDS

My dedication to exquisite words, couplets and all literary forms
started early in the country of my birth in the Mediterranean Sea
There is evidence A tiny black n' white rectangle photograph
depicting me as a four-year-old
on stage at Nicosia Town Hall in 1967
at an end-of-year school celebration

Just as I came off my *apagelma*
my older brother, all of seven, by my side, posing like he always did
when photographed turning his head in a lopsided way
It was a poem I had *recited* (closest verb I can find in English)
my cheeks still flushed with Winter heating
the stage-lights I fell in love

What hope for me to lead a normal life? A third-child
craving unadulterated attention to be foisted not the firstborn
Not the first son, nor the first daughter third forever
I sub-consciously gravitated towards any adult male
anyone who wanted to pay me *special* attention
First in fifth class, dead-cert to be School Captain for my final year

But it was not to be The eternal enemy decided to invade the island
a decision wiping away my efforts at Speech Nights, school concerts
Choir Band, where singularly, I played the mandolin left-handed

all those recitals full of visceral patriotic fervour
Se gnorizo apo tin opsin tou spathiou tin tromeri... There's a national anthem
Sing that at football matches   I wager everybody'd know the lyrics

Every goosebump-inducing syllable, the ferocity of the strength of words.
A refugee camp, multiple sexual *favours* for food and banana-flavoured milk
(can't drink the stuff now). A ferryboat to the Motherland, then Olympic
a short stay with distant relatives in the lush streets of Gladesville
Sydney, Australia in late 1974,   briefly Boronia and Putney Public Schools
subjected to daily torment and isolation then Marrickville Public

All within four months, supposedly learning English with Mr Moustacas
My fellow reffo Troen, incongruously wanted us to go on *Pot of Gold*
toiling away at structural drills, guessing the missing words
speaking to nobody   I had been forced to go mute
no chance of being selected to speak at school celebrations
words would not come out right. I put on weight   Was ridiculed

My only chance lay in library books - There was no money
to buy even a newspaper, nor pocket money to forego a paddle pop
parents remained mute   My tongue begun to un-twirl
my jaw realigned, lips vibrating, formulating tame syllables
Oh so nasal when compared to the sharp vowel sounds
diphthongs of demotic modern Greek

Branded a *recent arrival*   I could not escape special classes, forced
to spend inexorably long sessions with Mrs Smith who
everyone knew hated migrants but who'd peculiarly chosen to teach
Special English, sitting silently at her desk whilst a handful of us: me,
a Vietnamese girl, Lui the Chinese maths genius, a hot chick from
Czechoslovakia sat, bored to death doing decontextualized Comprehension

Filling in blanks with murderous intentions to escape given the chance.
I scored a part in *Lil Abner*   Then an ongoing role as Donny Osmond
The Kingsgrove North High version of the *Donny & Marie Show*
Dunno why/how I came to interview the *papier mache* lifesize statue
outside the Art Staff Room for the School Magazine
nor why I was gifted book vouchers and once, a Concise

Collins Dictionary as Second Prize in the School Literature Contest
another for the First Prize in Year 9, Year 10 French, Indonesian, Italian
Finding myself sitting next to the only other boy in Year 11 English 1
(There were 7 English classes in my year- Christmas 1962
must have had lots of blackouts in the southern suburbs).
It felt awkward for me, especially given I was shook

By unintentional erections
when my fellow brawny brainiac's hairy knee would accidentally
touch mine during Chaucer, 1984, John Donne tutorials given
by our Balmain-dwelling, chablis-swilling Mr Lowe
I could've kissed the painfully-polite ex-De La Salle lad
who joined our class of nerdy girls in Term 2 of Year 12

Who never attended the School Dance, pseudo-activists-on-wheels
declaring men, our generation, useless. One of the loudest girls
became an out-and-proud visual artist, another a hot shot
in the Premier's department, another a tetchy journalist entrenched
in alcohol and the *Bubble* of the Canberra Press Gallery
None of us famous   Like Travolta or Shakespeare or David Sylvian

By then I'd been exiled to the outer-western suburbs and books
borrowed from tiny Ingleburn Library kept me amused for the 2.5-hour
each way trip to and from school and to KFC where I worked
to contribute to our flailing budget. I spent New Year's Eve
at 18 stuck in an empty carriage at rough-as-guts Macquarie Fields Station
the driver, celebrating with his squeeze, was not in any great hurry

No one was more surprised than me when I matriculated
to the oldest university in the country   Joy was short-lived
having a wog accent, being male, did not, respectively, go down well
in law tutorials and literature ones in the Woolley Building   Too swarthy
to be allowed to speak, female students were the chosen ones
in the early 80s, even if diversity/inclusion had not yet become a thing

Three years focussed on privileged women authors from earlier centuries
who bore no relevance to my life
novels chosen by female lecturers
who could have used a bit of lipstick and mousse or a steam iron.
Caught in a rip of words I retreated to my mute state
tutors interpreted my disengagement as sullenness, male ethnic arrogance.

Disillusioned with prescribed readings I started acting in SUDS productions
spotted by the powerhouse Liz Mullinar who got me an agent   Bit parts
still finishing my first degree- what madness to believe I could be an actor
Me! A short, impoverished gay *ethnic.* Worked day and night
to survive, found time to write poems and short stories
miraculously validated by the editor of the University magazine

Who told me I was going to be a major writer, I had no choice
but to believe him, swallowing my lack of self-esteem
hoping not to choke in an ocean of trauma
All the mentors who'd come my way thus far
were only willing to mentor me for sexual favours
That had been my curse since I was in single digits

Found the courage to write longer and longer works
amassing a drawer of fiction, full of positive rejection slips
from top editors of the best publishing houses in the country.
What incandescent madness to try selling a gay love story
months before homosexuality was decriminalised in NSW
and to UQP seven years before it became legal in its home state.

Liberal heterosexual publishers politely wrote they loved my work
could not see a market for a narrator who was gay *and* ethnic
There was talk of a short story being broadcast on the ABC
through the mother of my housemate but it never happened
she was too busy escaping to her weekender in Bowral
to ever pick a recording date.

As I had always been a conscientious boy, I listened to advice
to move mountains to get my work in print in many unread journals
sent off countless poems and short stories single-handedly improving

Australia Post's profits at Erskineville. I'd be a millionaire
if I were given a dollar each time I was advised *poetry doesn't sell* or,
Only major writers can expect to have their short stories published

Within a decade of dogged persistence ten poems, two short stories
In Southerly, Overland, Westerly, Mattoid, Outrider, Social Alternatives,
Famous Reporter, Hobo, Antipodes, anthologies by Penguin and UQP
Another in the USA, Canada, Greece, two gay monthly magazines
All had featured my work   the ubiquitous Second Prize, twice,
I was becoming a published writer in an open sea of wannabees

Short-circuiting any possibility of settling down as I had nothing
to offer a high-achiever prospect, for no other type resonated.
Before I knew it I was in my late twenties   interest was waning
one foppish trick, after we had a quick fracas, said
"All the good men are already taken by our age".
My closeted gay agent was critical: I had to be less sensitive, more butch

Was told repeatedly there were no parts written for ethnic actors
that my voice was too gentle, too soft. Directors would tell me I read well
but that I would *stick out like a sore thumb* with my ethnic face and would be
an unhelpful distraction for the audience.
There were no ethnic parts on *The Restless Years* or *Sons & Daughters*
soon, my agent had to "let me go"

A painful slap in the face despite the cast award I had won playing
a near-naked Greek in an acclaimed stage production for six months
No other money had been made from my decade-long liaison enmeshed
in words spoken or written, just paltry amounts which did not even
cover my forty-five-minute weekly voice-class with Bill Pepper
in his tiny Glebe terrace   All his pussies running amok on my abdomen

Breathe deeper   Dig deeper   Dig Deeper
In Greek we say every setback leads to something better
plunge in at the deep end of the pool
sink into the voluminous depths of your soul
risk freezing to death for there is neither family or friend
you can reach out to help you keep warm

Recognisant of the fact I would forever be classified *the other*
on the periphery of the mainstream I went back to my alma mater
did an Honours year   Broke, I made the fateful error of paying
a German student to type up my last essay that he mangled jumping
from page to page as he was on Quaaludes   My chances of getting
a First gone   for it was for the lecturer who disliked me   called me

A wop fool   for not checking the typed essay, it was Schadenfreude
for him to bring my brilliant average down   I rewrote my thesis
as a book and Currency Press published it   decades later

it is still in many libraries   has been photocopied for free
even by teaching members of my own family.
Then the heavy thump on the head hit me: there'd never be any parts

Written for us ethnics so I penned a play for myself and three friends
chosen by the only company producing Australian work, the Griffin
For a showcase - thunderous applause   no producer picked the play up
a second effort was selected for a Week of New Plays at Belvoir
lots of genuine jubilant noise was made about a production
again, no telephone or telegram came through, no contract

With typical youthful exuberance   as if jet-skiing
believing that one man could change the status quo
I financed a production which sold out its five-week season,
garnered rave reviews, even on the ABC's *Sunday Arts* programme
with the main host   Ross Someone declaring
in 1990 plays such as mine were *the way of the future*

A self-proclaimed wannabe tv producer did contact me   Then
it became clear it wasn't my skills as a playwright or actor he sought
he replicated interest from other much older males, men of power
in the industry all of whom I had foolishly turned down
who did not take kindly to this   I could not flirt shamelessly
then play the "I'd love to but I'm straight" card like hetero actors

Powerful stakeholders never forgave me my obstinate slight
certainly never offered me a paying part   I fell off my jet-ski
I had had my share of abuse
did not wish to whore myself
evidently I was raised a strict Greek Orthodox obliging boy
Holy Communion meant something else to industry sharks

Back to teaching declension, the nominative, genitive accusative cases
for stickler Chinese students, the ubiquitous definite and indefinite articles
Can't recall how SBS threw me a lifeline asking me to write first one
then three scripts, two of which were broadcast without a word changed
the third, unrecognisable
some other dude given first screenwriting credit

My name credited second   apparently, the producer told me, my name
wasn't ethnic enough for the powers that be for funding
I was asked to change my name to make it more ethnic
so my nickname Icarus was brought out of storage and memory
gained when, aged 2, I jumped off the balcony onto Areos St below
My mother's palatial neo-classical maternal home in Old Nicosia

Breaking my collarbone, lived in silent isolation from other children
Icarus could not save me anymore than he had saved himself
I starved in my mould-infested Paddington flat, not having money

to even pay the entrance fee at Andrew Boy Charlton pool
where I diligently did my laps when I could afford it
spotting famous people sunning themselves, none of them ethnic

On one occasion even becoming intimate
with a television host one afternoon in the showers.
By this stage I had been working as a casual teacher for years
teaching first teenagers and then foreign students
the joys of the English language
whilst devising ways I could create another meaty role for myself

By writing another play   first I had to pay off the debt
accumulated by my previous theatrical triumph
Despite the acclaim, bums on seats, it still left me with a huge debt
I slowly repaid- others my age had a car loan or a European trip
I had perpetual loans to pay off   penance for the indulgence
Of diving head-in into words on the proscenium

I taught students tongue twisters, the perfect present tense continuous
helped them with TOEFL and IELTS   Got promoted
kept my volunteering up at Griffin and lo and behold my third play
chosen   A Week of New Plays
once more the feedback session provided a wonderful response
yet the artistic director didn't put their money where their mouth was

I doggedly became determined to present this play, about violence
towards gay men, those perceived as all around me gay bashings
were *di rigeur* a pastime for adolescents from the 'burbs who descended
into the city, to beats, literally threw gay men they lured over cliffs
bashed them in toilet blocks that had reputation as a place where gays
cruised for a moment of sexual acceptance

I too was punched and kicked on Darlinghurst Road one night
but in 1993 not even the gay ghetto was ready to embrace such a play
I was criticised by gay journalists for not depicting physical displays
of affection between teacher and his student
an abhorrent anathema give the morality imbued in me
given my personal history of abuse

The three years I'd spent lobbying Virginia Chadwick, the Department
my local MP Clover Moore, the exhaustive cajoling of hundreds of
English/Drama teachers by phone, letter, fax, meetings with teacher
associations, deputy-principals, virulent, overworked school admin
All these efforts did not register as significant in the amateur world
of unpaid gay journalists who also outed me, involuntarily

Holding my head under water
the oppressed make the worst oppressors
severing ties with my parents.

It wasn't until 2016 that SBS produced a documentary
about these same gay bashings   I'll take comfort in the fact
that I was *avant-garde*   like Rainer Werner Fassbinder

At 33, defeated like Jesus, I nevertheless scored an agent,
the great Hilary Linstead told me she was "watching" me
top agents had seen my bashing play and wooed me
in hindsight, I chose the wrong agent: I liked the history
that agency had, but they were milking past successes
of authors who were no longer signed with them

The agent, like most, was Machiavellian only for her own success
She dropped me shortly after I left Sydney, destitute, post cancer.
Basically, she arranged one meeting for me with a publisher
in fourteen years, who told me straight-faced that
"We've already got one Greek-Australian male writer on our books"
as if that were sufficient reasoning for such overt systemic racism

One wog is enough/all wogs are the same/ all gay writers are the same...
My anger has still not subsided decades later
I've never relied on the *professional ethnic* card to earn my stripes
breaking through any number of glass ceilings without medical care.
For decades I have been underestimated, invalidated and forgotten
retreating to imaginary words as they offered salvation, a hiding place

Managing university English language centres where adults paid me
to teach them language for their own success whilst my own stagnated
became a distant past   Twenty-five years had lapsed since my Honours
Second Class Division II graduation (73%) Dozens of publications amassed
More university qualifications on student loans demanded by my position
Finally, a small but prolific poetry publisher said yes to my modest collection

The buzz of proofreading on my lunchbreak, spacing corrections at night
talking cover design, writing a biography, choosing a cover
finally holding the slim volume in my hand   rivers of tears
joy, on account of seeing my words in print
a cheque for twenty-six dollars after two hundred copies
were sold, proving I was not commercially lucrative, like David Leavitt

How many times do I HAVE TO BE LET GO?
I refuse to let go damn you!
The Lord giveth   The Lord taketh
I figured a new book out was penance for Surviving Stage Four
Cancer   Everyone begrudged me surviving, initial caring gives way to
resentment and caring fatigue. No reviews ensued.

One day, I accidentally unearthed my childhood stamp album
that somehow mother had usurped from the Turks
These miniature works of art reawakened my creative dreams

only my carefully-chosen brutal words were needed to turn
what I thought was the story of my life into a narrative I could
leave behind for anyone who cared or wondered, *Whatever happened to Luke?*

Decades in the rice fields of debt   avoided HIV but got NHL
more treatment, infections, anonymity   no one gave me a cent
Remission living in borrowed rooms   The Adelaide foothills
Proofreading others' words for some pennies interspersed
with road trips to Sydney to the production company facilities
editing the 35mm short completed with determination and favours.

Back to a quiet life before garnering the gumption to contact creatives
who'd heaped enthusiastic praise on my younger self
(God Bless you Robyn K.)   Months later, out of the blue an email
which lead to another email, which lead to selling the film to the ABC
five screenings in exchange for three weeks' rent, great pride in seeing
my name as the writer, director, co-producer, editor, the star of the film

Take that you   whoever rejected me   egomaniac shit lovers
publishers, editors, acting agents, literary agents,
directors, producers, Anglo-Saxon casting people, NIDA panel
No calls came after the screening. No offers. Not even as a token ethnic
fruit and vegetable owner   or a one-liner cameo as the criminal
I felt as if I were pushed from a cliff, crashing onto the sea rocks below

Devotion to the vocational education of others subsumed my energy
making money for institutions that'd never seen a Balance Sheet in the black
First Australian to negotiate a major tertiary contract in South America
my laptop had to be thrown out on account of the keyboard being so worn
Words poured out of me in the evenings
sizeable slippery seals diving into an ice-covered Arctic sea

On the weekends too, no day was off-limit, even Christmas Days
some spent alone others with family asking *Are you still writing?*
Once on Somers Beach with A. where we fell asleep in the glorious sun
sleepy from champagne and love woke up the colour of lobsters
Still, the experience, brought us together emotionally
so much so that I agreed to co-pen a book on smoking with him

It sold out in Melbourne
did not do too badly elsewhere
after distribution fees we made less than $100 each- it'd cost us
thousands (they saw us coming), an imprint of a boutique
prestigious high-end publisher who were not the least interested
in even reading my more literary efforts as their *list was full*

My ma and pa poetry publishers got sick, retired
I came to some arrangement with a dubious publisher whereby the cost risk
was totally mine. On New Year's Day I read they'd gone into liquidation

their assets frozen   all books with their ISBNs pulled
my books disappeared.
I worked doggedly   republished them under my own imprint

Chose better typesetting, higher quality of paper, made dozens of corrections
other writers started sending me manuscripts, desperate for publication
I knew publishing serious literature existed to enrich the cultural
landscape of an illiterate society that overlooks the power of words.
I challenge anyone to tell me those books were not presented
as parcels full of beautiful words wishing to be savoured

Illness   words   penury
my constant companions
I've never enjoyed the fruits of a double-income household
Forced to sell my inner-city home, my second-hand car
find solace in half-remembered words of encouragement
Professor Leonie Kramer   Noel Rowe   director Neil Armfield

I paid for three surgeries   moved five times in five years
need to now move again.   Where does a neglected bachelor
afflicted with several medical conditions move to exactly
without a regular income?
The first thing I pack are books
making sure the edges of the covers are not torn or damaged

The hundred or so Currency Press plays I proudly own I have stored
in the shed, too painful seeing them with their red blot on the spine
reminding me of all my unproduced, unheard, unseen plays
edited and re-drafted a dozen times.
The long-awaited novel that I delve into at times of hope and defeat
requires an agent to sell it to a worthwhile publisher

As time catches up on me (everyone who thought I had any talent is dead)
every decade since my birth there has been a crisis of sorts in my quiet life
war, refugee camp and migration in 1974   graduation from university in 1984
1994 leaving my job at Sydney Uni, fleeing to the Motherland
Leaving my second uni job after eighteen months of chemo in 2004
Leaving my Principal's job exactly ten years later, 2014 as blood pressure hit 170

Words have been demanded of me: stock phrases, relative, non-relative clauses
phrasal verbs, colloquialisms, curricula, manifestos, syllabi, slang even
systematic office procedures, equitable HR policies, staff employment
contracts, teports for the VC, various DVCs, Rectors and boards
politically correct texts across all the latest communication platforms
to ensure inclusivity, gender-neutral fairness and superficial diversity

Dozens and dozens of uncredited corporate scripts and digital content
every paid gig has presumed I'm a wordsmith, a consummate orator
(you try MC-ing monthly graduation ceremonies in the far-western suburbs)

where I had to be feign heterosexuality so as not to offend other cultures
a long time since someone on the bus called out to my mum in Top Ryde
Stop rabbiting on in that dago lingo decades ago

We migrants were often reminded of our place
seems the universe is forcing me to make a choice
every ten years: choose words and life or financial survival
Why does it seem I've made the wrong choice each time
opting for words,   words that failed to reward my account
costing me more than a cocaine habit

Although admittedly sometimes my wordiness brings me a smile
a nephew once declared I spoke just like Niles from *Frasier*
another time at Belvoir St Theatre
a visiting American producer said my words
made her laugh and cry simultaneously
(but I am 60 now   an occasional smile won't do, pet)

Allowed to marry at 54; this age equals a long-dead fossil
in the battered gay ghetto. Every single one of my lovers
(mostly Italian Mamma's pretty boys)
a Spaniard who kept me as insurance in a safety deposit box for decades
uber-butch closeted Greeks, my brooding Chilean maths professor
pitch black eyes with eyelashes like Carlotta on stage in her heyday

Has at some stage, laughingly or seriously
sometimes in the middle of making love to themselves,
complained I read too much   am too cerebral to be found
flippantly gay
(no other type is allowed in society)
that I should read more commercial fiction

I should consider writing softcore erotica or write more formulaic
target-market books, romance fiction, bestsellers like Liane Moriarty
declaring me *dramatic* – clearly not intending me to infer it as a compliment.
No, marriage equality came far too late to benefit my generation
anyhow, I would look somewhat creepy now in red Speedos   *At his age!*
fishing in the riverbank of flirting with fit, lithe *twunks*

Gliding through the crystalline water   battling blue bottles
currents, undertows, stingrays, the jellyfish of my distant youth
lamentably, hypertension forbids me to fathom the strength
to play lifesaver   *Malheureusement*
specimens of coveted masculinity elude me   swipe past me
sensuality only for the young, who swim ahead of me in the lane

A not-in-demand red mullet
since our arrival in the verdant avenues on the Hunters Hill
border   all six of us living in one room

sharing a dilapidated single bathroom
with a family of seven   My Good Lord!
Was it just for the month, before we rented an empty fibro house?

How utterly unsexy to be shivering at my age
the Daikin air-conditioner remains switched off
to keep warm in Blackheath's Winter you need money
a truckload of firewood
costs more than my fortnightly income
lasts merely a week

To keep your cool in a Riverina summer
you need more than a gig economy income
there is nobody to reach out to for a helping hand.
How ingloriously humiliating it is to be irrelevant
invisible   all through your late 50s   on your own
at 60   even my dog has died

It is a final slap   this forced move to the country
six hundred kilometres from the streets I've known
that's what happens when you're on a single haphazard
artist's income   isolated from known landscapes, people
amenities like health, food, public transport, entertainment,
erotic entanglements, dalliances: I haven't flirted with a soul in years.

Another play written explicitly requiring diverse actors
another demanding main role to play   domestic violence
in a well-renowned theatre in Melbourne   After COVID postponements
we play in a half-empty space observing the distancing and mask laws
of the Socialist Dictator _ two and a half hours on stage
for what ? Not even for minimum union salary.

Still, my frozen lake shimmers like the swimming pools
in Hockney's larger Californian canvases, angling to reflect a rainbow
I fear I shall remain a male Ophelia, underwater forever
only a vague hope delicious, supercilious trout might break through
rise to the surface   the iridescent light   any day now
this rivulet might start to break waves, become a rugged sea.

ACKNOWLEDGEMENTS

Some of the poems in this collection have been previously published in earlier versions in the following literary journals, books and anthologies:

In *Southerly*:

- The Crimes of A Simple Man
- Love Latino Style
- The Man Was Something Like The Title Of An ABBA Song
- Taste It
- My Cancer Tastes Like A *Fresita*
- Night Omens
- Vital Lie
- Paradise Is Full Of Supporting Roles
- Resignation
- The Princess Mary
- Madonna
- All of these poems also appeared in the collection, *Latin*

In *Mattoid*:

- Some Men
- Abuse

In *Westerly*:

- Dangling Dice

In *Social Alternatives*:

- Wound

In *Antipodes:*

- Next Of Kin

In *Hobo*

- Cape of Good Hope

In The Cabinet of Lost & Found, Sydney Writers' Festival:

- Tracing History On An Island Far From Your Desert

In *The Poetry of Men's Lives,* University of Georgia Press

- Measuring Apollo
- Ravine

In the Greek journal, *Akti*

- Clarity In Herod Atticus Street

In the book, *The Transit Of Cancer*:

- Neurotic Bachelor
- I Recall One Christmas
- Family Lunch Interstate
- Last Prayer
- Easter Island
- Moving Back With Father As A Middle-Aged Single Man

In the film, *My Stamp Collection*

- The Politics of Dying

Printed in the USA
CPSIA information can be obtained
at www.ICGtesting.com
LVHW040353120924
790640LV00008B/983

9 780994 518262